delicious hearty one-pot cooking recipes

slow cook

D1462938

Contents

Introduction	3
Beef	7
Chicken	23
Fish	43
Lamb	51
Pork	59
Vegetables	73
Desserts	85
Index	95

Text by Sara Burford.

This edition published in 2008 by L&K Designs.
© L&K Designs 2008
PRINTED IN CHINA

Publishers Disclaimer

The recipes contained in this book are passed on in good faith but the publisher cannot be held responsible for any adverse results. Please be aware that certain recipes may contain nuts.

Introduction

Slow Cooker or Crockpot?

Ever wondered what the difference is between a slow cooker and a crockpot? There actually isn't any difference. A 'Crock-pot' is a brand name borne in the 1970's, which slow cookers generically adopted as their namesake. There are now a wide variety of different brands, styles, shapes and sizes of slow cookers – but the name 'Crock-pot' is still popular as a 'fits-all' term.

What's So Great about Slow Cooking?

Time & Space

Whether you're a busy parent running yourself ragged at home, or whether you're working a full-time career, juggling bringing up kids alongside a job...or just plain old tired of feeling like an eternal slave to your kitchen, and wanting to create more time to do the things that are important to you...slow cookers are a great way of giving you time and space, without the hassle and worry of having to fuss over making a meal in the evening.

And what a great way to cook – 'bung it all in' and leave the slow cooker to do its stuff! Of course, there are some recipes which need a little more attention than others – but even then, once the ingredients are prepared and in, there's little more you need to do than wait for the fantastic meal that will be ready at the end of cooking time.

Good Wholesome Food

With the rising tide of health concerns raised by poor nutrition and unhealthy eating habits, we're starting to move away from the novelty that the fast-food and pre-packaged industries has had us buying-into over the past few decades. Slow cooking takes us back to using more wholesome foods and less processed ingredients.

There's no drying-out, no ferocious cooking and bubbling, no killing all the goodies and nutrients in food, (no death-by-boiling which was so popular in my mother's era!), and the tastes that come from this gentle and slow way of cooking are absolutely divine!

Economic

Cooking for 8 hours? Isn't that a bit irresponsible in our environment-conscious climate? Well, you can rest easy on that one. The average slow cooker uses less electricity than a light bulb – so it's good to your bank balance too!

No More 'Your Dinner's in the Dog'

Does your household have a perpetually late-for-dinner husband, wife or teenager? Does it drive you to distraction having worked hard at preparing a meal, only for it to be ruined within minutes of putting it in the oven to keep it warm? And microwaving a meal never restores it to its former glory. Infuriating!

Slow cookers are fantastically forgiving in this respect and will keep things warm for up to 30 minutes, without ruining the meal. In fact, most recipes will stand cooking for up to an hour longer on a low temperature, should it be deemed necessary - casseroles in particular are great for this! Do be careful of ingredients such as rice though, as the rice will go sticky when overcooked.

Slow Cooker Tips

Before you get going on your slow cooking expedition, here are a few pointers before you begin...

- If you've never used your slow cooker before, ensure that you read ALL the manufacturer's instructions.

- Generally cooking temperatures fall within a similar range for most slow cookers, but some may differ enough to make a difference to your cooking times. This information will be held within your slow cooker's instruction booklet/leaflet.

- Take a careful note of the individual care and personal safety requirements of your slow cooker.

- Preheating slow cookers is not usually necessary, but will depend very much on the make of the product. For clarity, read the manufacturer's instructions – as some products also warn against preheating whilst empty.

- During cooking the outer lid of your slow cooker will get scorching hot – so use heat resistant gloves when handling. Refer to your slow cooker's safety instructions.

- Slow cooking is fantastic at drawing out the succulent tastes of meat and chicken – it's also very good at drawing out fats, so it's a good idea to skim the surface of your dishes before serving. You can do this by using a spoon, paper kitchen towel or a fat-sucking utensil, (designed for just the job!)

- Slow cookers generally retain heat for at least 30 minutes once switched off, so your meal won't get cold if you're not quite ready at the end of cooking time.

- Hot or boiling liquids will speed up cooking time, (where liquids have been specified).

- Salt will draw the moisture from your dishes, so add it at the end of cooking – unless otherwise specified.

- Avoid lifting the lid during cooking where possible, i.e. only lift the lid if the recipe specifies it. Lifting the lid releases heat and moisture from the slow cooker, which is essential for this cooking method.

Slow Cooker Pots 'N' Stuff

The vast majority of recipes will be housed perfectly by the inner ceramic cooking pot, which fits snugly inside the slow cooker – however, sometimes you will need to use other kitchen equipment to accommodate particular recipes, such as cake and dessert recipes. These will include:-

Ramekins
Soufflé dishes
Cake tins
Square & rectangular baking tins
Dariole moulds
Pudding bowls
Terrines
Loaf tins

Before you use any new equipment in your slow cooker you'll need to check that the equipment:-

Fits! Both in width and depth
Is watertight
Is heat resistant

These might seem like obvious pointers, but it's easy to get yourself geared up for a good old-fashioned cooking session, to suddenly realise that you can't get the slow cooker lid on the gorgeous soufflé you've just prepared! Better to be safe than sorry – and left tearing your hair out!

Beef

Beef & 4-Bean Chili (Serves 6-8)

Ingredients

450g/2 cups of minced beef
400g/6½ cups of canned pinto beans (drained)
400g/6½ cups of canned kidney beans (drained)
400g/6½ cups of canned dark red kidney beans (drained)
400g/6½ cups of canned hot chili beans (drained)
300g salsa (mild or hot, dependant on taste)
75g/½ cup of onion (chopped)
1 clove of garlic (crushed)
½ tsp slow chilies

Method

1. Cook at a low temperature. Heat a frying pan over a medium heat and add the minced beef, garlic and chopped onion. Cook for 3-5 minutes until the beef is browned. Transfer to the slow cooker.

2. Add the rest of the ingredients to the slow cooker and cook for 7 to 9 hours. Serve with rice.

Beef & Autumn Vegetable Stew (Serves 8)

Ingredients

900g stewing beef (cubed)
875g/5 cups of potatoes (peeled & diced)
3 slices of bacon (diced)
225g/1½ cups of onion (chopped)
3 celery sticks (finely chopped)
3 carrots (sliced)
300g/2 cups of swede (diced)
675ml/3 cups of beef broth
225ml/1 cup of apple cider
3 tbsp flour
2 bay leaves
1 tsp dried rosemary (crushed)
½ tsp mixed herbs
3 tbsp water
Salt & black pepper (to season)
1 tbsp fresh parsley (chopped)

Method

1. Cook at a low temperature. Heat a large frying pan over a medium heat and add the bacon, cubed beef and onions.

2. Cook for 4-5 minutes, until the beef is lightly browned and the bacon is cooked.

3. Transfer the slow cooker and add the potatoes, carrots, beef broth, celery, swede, apple cider, bay leaves and herbs. Combine all the ingredients well.

4. Cover and cook for 7 to 9 hours, until the beef is tender.

5. Place the flour and water in a mixing jug and stir until smooth. Add to the slow cooker, stirring well. Increase the temperature to high and cook for a further 20 minutes.

Beef

Beef & Beer Stew (Serves 8)

Ingredients

1.75kg topside beef roast (trimmed & cubed)
1 onion (chopped)
2 celery sticks (chopped)
2 carrots (sliced)
2-3 large potatoes (cubed)
375ml/1 & 2/3 cup of beef broth
225ml/1 cup of beer
60g/½ cup of flour
1½ tsp paprika
2 tbsp vegetable oil
1 tsp salt
½ tsp black pepper

Method

1. Cook at a low temperature. Place the flour, salt, black pepper and paprika in a bowl and mix together. Coat the beef cubes in the mixture.

2. Heat the oil in a large frying pan and add the beef. Cook for 4-6 minutes, until the meat is lightly browned.

3. Place the vegetables in the slow cooker and season with the remaining salt and black pepper. Top with the beef.

9

Beef & Beer Stew/Cont.

4. Combine the beer and beef broth and add to the slow cooker. Cover and cook for 7 to 9 hours

5. Place the flour and water in a mixing jug and stir until smooth. Add to the slow cooker, stirring well. Increase the temperature to high and cook for a further 20 minutes.

Beef Stir-Fry (Serves 8)

Ingredients
900g beef blade steak (trimmed & cut into thin slices)
20 spears of asparagus (trimmed and cut into thirds)
2 tsp sesame oil
1 clove of garlic (crushed)
225ml/1 cup of barbeque sauce
3 tsp fresh ginger (grated)
4 tbsp soy sauce
Toasted pine nuts
1 tbsp vegetable oil

Method

1. Cook at a low temperature. Heat the vegetable oil and add the sliced steak pieces and garlic.

2. Cook quickly on a high heat until the meat is browned on all sides. Transfer to the slow cooker, without the excess oil/fat.

3. Add the ginger, soy sauce, barbeque sauce and sesame oil and mix all the ingredients together. Cover and cook for 7 to 8 hours, stirring halfway through cooking.

4. Half an hour before the end of cooking, add the asparagus and cook for the remaining time. Serve sprinkled with roasted pine nuts.

Beef Curry (Serves 8)

Ingredients

1.5kg beef (cubed)
3 onions (sliced)
900g/4 cups of canned chopped tomatoes (drained)
2 cloves of garlic (crushed)
330ml/1½ cups of beef broth
3 tbsp olive oil
60g/½ cup of flour
400g jarred Silverskin onions (chopped)
1 tsp paprika
1 tsp salt
½ tsp black pepper
2 tbsp curry powder (or to taste)

Method

1. Cook at a low temperature. Place the flour, salt and paprika in a bowl and mix together well. Coat the beef cubes in the mixture.

2. Heat the oil in a large frying pan and add the beef, followed by the sliced onions. Cook for 5-6 minutes until the beef is lightly browned and onions are tender. Transfer to the slow cooker.

3. Pour the beef broth into the slow cooker, followed by the tomatoes, Silverskin onions and curry powder.

4. Cover and cook for 7 to 9 hours, until the beef is tender. Serve with rice and a side salad.

Corned Beef Hash & Cheese Casserole (Serves 3-4)

Ingredients

900g frozen hash browns (shredded)
150g/1½ cups of cheddar cheese (grated)
75g/½ cup of finely chopped onion
1 can of cream of celery soup
2 cups of canned corned beef (mashed)
110ml/½ cup of evaporated milk
2 tsp celery seeds
Salt & pepper (to season)

Method

1. Spray the slow cooker with non-stick cooking spray, or lightly grease with butter. Cook at a low temperature.

2. Place about ¼ of the shredded hash browns at the bottom of the slow cooker, followed by 1/3 of the chopped onion, 1/3 of the corned beef and 1/3 of the cheese. Add 1/3 of the celery seed and seasoning.

3. Repeat this layering sequence twice more and end with a layer of potato, sprinkled over with grated cheese, celery seed and seasoning.

4. Place the evaporated milk and soup in a mixing jug and combine. Pour into the slow cooker.

5. Cover and cook for 8 to 9 hours.

Mexican-Style Meatloaf (Serves 4-6)

Ingredients
500g minced beef
225g sausage meat
1 onion (finely chopped)
395g refried beans
2 eggs, beaten
130g tomato puree
1 tbsp Mexican chilli powder

Method

1. Spray the inside of the slow cooker with a non-stick cooking spray. Place the minced beef, sausage meat, tomato puree, onion, chilli powder, eggs and refried beans and mix together well.

2. Press the mixture into the slow cooker. Cover and cook on a low temperature for 7 to 8 hours.

3. Once cooked, leave to cool a little for 20 minutes before running a knife around the edge of the meatloaf to loosen it. Turn out onto a board.

4. Cut into slices to serve. Serve hot or cold, either on it's own or as a tortilla-filling.

Chili Beef (Serves 6-8)

Ingredients

900g/4 cups of minced beef
900g/4 cups of canned chopped tomatoes
250g sliced green chilies (finely chopped)
2 cloves of garlic (crushed)
150g/1 cup of onion (chopped)
$\frac{3}{4}$ tbsp dried oregano
1 tbsp chili powder

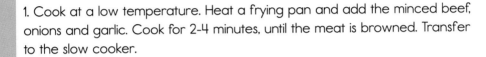

Method

1. Cook at a low temperature. Heat a frying pan and add the minced beef, onions and garlic. Cook for 2-4 minutes, until the meat is browned. Transfer to the slow cooker.

2. Add the remaining ingredients and mix together well. Cover and cook for 7 to 9 hours. Serve in tacos with accompaniments such as guacamole, soured cream and salsa.

Beef Stroganoff (Serves 4-6)

Ingredients

675g steak (cut into strips)
1 onion (chopped)
1 clove of garlic (crushed)
175g canned sliced mushrooms (drained)
2 beef bouillon cubes
225ml/1 cup of sour cream
225ml/1 cup of water
30g/¼ cup of flour
½ tsp salt
¼ tsp black pepper

Method

1. Cook at a low temperature. Mix all of the ingredients, (with the exception of the sour cream), together in a bowl and transfer to the slow cooker.

2. Cover and cook for 8 to 9 hours. Add the sour cream 15 minutes before the end of cooking, (if ready to serve), and gently stir in well. Cook for 15 minutes and serve with hot rice.

Beef

Hot Beef & Vegetables with Horseradish (Serves 6)

Ingredients

6 x 180g braising steaks
16 small shallots (peeled & halved)
560ml/2½ cups of hot beef stock
2½ tbsp plain flour
150g/1 cup of baby carrots (chopped)
2 bay leaves
1 clove of garlic (crushed)
2½ tbsp creamed horseradish
¼ tsp ground ginger
2 tsp molasses
1 tbsp Worcestershire sauce
1½ tsp curry powder
2 tbsp vegetable oil
Salt & black pepper (to season)

Method

1. Sprinkle the flour onto a large plate and season with salt and black pepper. Coat each of the braising steaks in the flour. Cook at a high temperature.

2. Heat the vegetable oil in a large frying pan and add the steaks. Cook on a high heat, browning both sides of the steaks. Transfer the steaks to the slow cooker.

3. Place the shallots in the still-hot frying pan and cook over a medium heat for 8-10 minutes, until golden brown and softening.

4. Add the ginger, curry powder and garlic and cook for a further 1-2 minutes.

5. Transfer to the slow cooker, spreading the shallot mixture over the meat. Sprinkle over the top with the molasses.

6. Pour in the beef stock, followed by carrots, horseradish, Worcestershire sauce and bay leaf. Mix all of the ingredients together and season with salt and black pepper, according to taste.

7. Cover and cook for 1 hour.

8. Reduce the slow cooker to a low temperature and cook for a further 6 to 7 hours, until the beef and vegetables are tender.

9. Remove the bay leaf before serving, and sprinkle with salt and black pepper.

Beef in Red Wine with Dumplings (Serves 4)

Ingredients Stew:

450g lean stewing beef (cubed)
6 mushrooms (sliced)
2 carrots (sliced)
1 celery stick (sliced)
1 onion (sliced)
110ml/½ cup of dry red wine
225g/1 cup of canned chopped tomatoes
15g/1/8 cup of flour
30ml/1/8 cup of water
¾ tsp salt
1/8 tsp black pepper
½ tsp dry mustard
½ tsp dried thyme leaves

Ingredients Dumplings:

60g/½ cup of shredded suet
150g/1 cups of self-raising flour
¾ tbsp parsley (finely chopped)
Salt & black pepper (to season)
Water (for mixing)

Stew:

1. Cook at a low temperature. Place all of the stew ingredients, (with the exception of the flour and water), in the slow cooker and mix together.

2. Cover and cook for 9 to 10 hours, until the beef and vegetables are tender.

3. Place the water and flour in a bowl and mix together until smooth. Stir into the slow cooker.

Dumplings:

4. Sieve the flour into a bowl, followed by the suet, parsley, salt and pepper. Add about 3 tablespoons of water, enough to make a soft, (but not sticky), dough.

5. Flour a work surface and your hands and roll the dough into 6-8 small balls. Add to the stew.

6. Increase the slow cooker temperature to a high setting and cook for a further 20 to 40 minutes.

Steak and Kidney Pie (Serves 4)

Ingredients
675g stewing steak (trimmed & cubed)
225g lamb's kidney (trimmed & cubed)
2 onions (chopped)
2¼ tbsp plain flour
3 tbsp vegetable oil
300ml/1 & 1/3 cup of beef stock
1 tbsp unsalted butter
1 tbsp tomato puree
380g puff pastry
1 egg (beaten)
2 tsp English mustard
1 tbsp fresh parsley (chopped)
Salt & black pepper (to season)

Method

1. Cook at a high temperature. Heat 2 tbsp of the vegetable oil in a frying pan and add the stewing steak. Cook gently until lightly browned.

2. Remove from the frying pan with a spoon, (without the fat from the pan), and transfer to the slow cooker.

3. Add the kidney to the frying pan and cook gently for 2-3 minutes, until lightly browned. Transfer to the slow cooker.

Steak and Kidney Pie/Cont.

4. Place the butter and the remaining vegetable oil in the frying pan and melt. Add the onions and cook for 4-5 minutes, until softened. Sprinkle in the flour and cook for 1 minute, stirring continuously. Remove from the heat.

5. Stir in the beef stock, followed by the mustard and tomato puree. Return the pan to the heat and bring to the boil, stirring continuously. Once the gravy has thickened, pour over the meat in the slow cooker. Season the gravy with salt and black pepper and stir well. Cover and cook for 6 to 7 hours, until the meat is tender.

6. During the cooking time, roll out the puff pastry and cut out a 10 inch round, (using a dinner plate to cut around). Place on a baking tray, lined with baking parchment.

Spiced Beef in Guinness (Serves 4-6)

Ingredients
1.75kg joint of silverside beef
335ml/1½ cups of Guinness
1 onion (finely chopped)
2 bay leaves (crushed)
1 tbsp ground allspice
1 tsp ground cloves
1 tbsp coarsely ground black pepper
1 tbsp juniper berries (crushed)
1½ tsp ginger
2½ tbsp dark brown sugar

Method

1. Two to three days before cooking, firstly prepare the beef. Place the sugar, spices and black pepper in a bowl and mix together well. Rub thoroughly into the beef joint.

2. Place the crushed bay leaves and chopped onion in a bowl and mix together. Rub the mixture into the beef.

3. Place the joint in a lidded container and keep in the refrigerator for 2-3 days. Turn the joint and rub in the mixture daily.

4. When ready to cook, remove from the fridge and place in the slow cooker. Cover the joint with cold water, (only just covering the top).

5. Cover and cook on a high temperature for 4 hours, until the meat is tender. Add the Guinness to the slow cooker 1 hour before the end of cooking.

6. Once cooked, leave to cool before removing from the slow cooker. Either serve warm, or cool completely and wrap in foil wrap and refrigerate.

Three-Spice Brisket (Serves 5-6)

Ingredients
900g brisket
1 can of French onion soup
55ml/¼ cup of water
30g/1/8 cup of tomato ketchup
1 clove of garlic (crushed)
¼ tsp black pepper
¼ tsp ground cinnamon
¼ tsp ground allspice
1/8 tsp ground ginger
1 tbsp Worcestershire sauce
1 tbsp flour
3 tbsp cold water

Method

1. Cook at a low temperature. Place the brisket in the slow cooker. Place the ¼ cup of water, soup, spices, garlic, pepper and Worcestershire sauce in a bowl and mix together well. Add to the slow cooker.

2. Cover and cook for 8 to 10 hours. Remove the brisket from the slow cooker and skim any fat from the gravy.

Three-Spice Brisket/Cont.

3. Place 1 tablespoon of flour and 3 tablespoons of water in a bowl and mix together until smooth. Gradually, stir into the slow cooker and cook for a further 20 to 25 minutes.

4. Slice the brisket to serve and spoon over with some of the spiced gravy.

Chicken

Artichoke Hearts & Chicken (Serves 8)

Ingredients

900g chicken breasts (skinless & chopped)
300g/1 & 1/3 cup of artichoke hearts
225ml/1 cup of chicken broth
300g/4 cups of mushrooms (sliced)
450g/2 cups of canned chopped tomatoes
75g/½ cup of onion (chopped)
75g pitted black olives (halved)
60ml/1/3 cup of dry white wine
2 tsp curry powder
3 tbsp quick-cook tapioca
Salt & black pepper (to season)
½ tsp thyme (crushed)

Method

1. Cook at a low temperature. Place the artichoke hearts, chicken broth, olives, onion, wine, mushrooms and tomatoes in the slow cooker and mix together.

2. Stir in the curry powder, thyme, tapioca and season with the salt and pepper. Add the chicken, spooning the mixture over the top.

3. Cover with the lid and place in the oven for 6-8 hours. Serve with hot cooked rice.

Chicken a la King (Serves 8)

Ingredients

8 cooked chicken breasts (skinless & diced)
620ml/2¾ cups of cream of mushroom soup
225g canned sliced mushrooms (drained)
110g/¾ cup of onion (chopped)
100g/1 cup of celery (finely chopped)
85g/½ cup of green pepper (finely chopped)
375g/2½ cup of frozen peas
100g pimento pepper (chopped)

Method

1. Cook at a low temperature. Place all the ingredients, (except the frozen peas), in the slow cooker and combine well.

2. Cover and cook for 6 to 7 hours. Add the peas 40 minutes before the end of cooking and turn the oven up to a medium heat.

Chicken Cacciatore (Serves 4)

Ingredients

4 chicken breasts (skinless & diced)
1 onion (chopped)
845g/3¾ cups of canned chopped tomatoes
225g/3 cups of mushrooms (sliced)
1 green pepper (chopped)
1 tbsp Italian herb seasoning
1 clove of garlic (crushed)
Pinch of red pepper flakes

Method

1. Cook at a low temperature. Place all the ingredients in a slow cooker and gently mix together. Cover and cook for 7-8 hours, until the chicken is cooked through.

2. Serve with pasta and sprinkle with Parmesan cheese.

Chicken Casserole & Wild Rice (Serves 6)

Ingredients

6 chicken breasts (skinless & diced)
1 can of cream of chicken soup
225g/3 cups of mushrooms (sliced)
75g diced bacon
225g/1 cup of long grain wild rice
225ml/1 cup of water
1 tbsp vegetable oil
1 tsp butter
1 tsp mixed herbs
Salt & black pepper (to season)

Method

1. Cook at a low temperature. Heat the butter and oil in a frying pan and add the chicken and mushrooms. Sauté until the chicken is lightly browned.

2. Place the bacon in the bottom of the slow cooker, followed by the rice. Add the chicken and mushrooms and pour in the soup and water.

3. Sprinkle over the mixed herbs and season with salt and black pepper, according to taste. Cover and cook for 5 to 6 hours, until the rice is cooked.

Chicken Curry (Serves 4-6)

Ingredients
4 chicken breasts (skinless & diced)
110ml/½ cup of chicken broth
1 onion (chopped)
2 cloves of garlic (crushed)
¼ tsp cinnamon
½ tsp cumin
½ tsp turmeric
½ tsp crushed red pepper flakes
¼ ground cardamom
2 tbsp cornstarch
2 tbsp cold water
1 tbsp fresh ginger (grated)
Pinch of ground cloves

Method

1. Cook at a low temperature. Place the onion, garlic, spices and seasonings in the slow cooker and mix together. Add the diced chicken and pour over the chicken broth.

2. Cover and cook for 6 to 7 hours, until the chicken is cooked through and tender. Transfer the chicken pieces only into a warm serving dish. Keep warm.

3. Increase the slow cooker temperature to high. Mix the cornstarch with the cold water and stir into the cooked liquid.

4. Cook until the sauce thickens, (stir every 5-7 minutes). Once the sauce has thickened pour over the chicken and serve with hot rice.

Chicken Enchilada Crockpot (Serves 8)

Ingredients
8 cooked chicken breasts (skinless & diced)
350g/2 cups of canned sweet corn (drained)
100g green chili peppers (chopped)
2 jars of enchilada sauce
9 corn tortillas
200g/2 cups of grated Cheddar cheese
400g/6½ cups of black beans (rinsed & drained)
1 tsp chili powder
¼ tsp ground black pepper
Sour cream or guacamole (to serve)

Method

1. Cook at a low temperature. Spray the slow cooker with cooking spray and place 3 of the tortillas in the bottom of the slow cooker.

2. Add the sweet corn, half of the chili peppers and seasonings and half of the chicken. Pour over ¾ cup of the enchilada sauce and sprinkle over half of the grated cheese.

3. Place 3 more tortillas over the top and add the black beans, remaining chili peppers, seasoning, chicken and cheese.

4. Place the remaining tortillas over the top and add the rest of the enchilada sauce. Cover and cook for 6 hours. Serve with guacamole and sour cream.

Chicken & Potato Crockpot with Butter Beans (Serves 8)

Ingredients
8 chicken breasts (skinless)
450ml/2 cups of chicken broth
4 large potatoes (cut into 1 inch pices)
375g/5 cups of canned butter beans
1½ tbsp vegetable oil
½ tsp thyme (crumbled)
Salt & pepper (to season)
½ tbsp butter

Method

1. Cook at a low temperature. Season the uncooked chicken with salt and pepper.

2. Heat the butter and vegetable oil in a large frying pan and add the chicken breasts. Cook over a medium heat until brown in both sides.

3. Place the remaining ingredients in the slow cooker and combine well. Add the browned chicken breasts and cook for 4 to 6 hours, until the chicken is cooked through.

Chicken and Mushroom Bake (Serves 4)

4 chicken breasts (skinless & cubed)
1 carrot (finely chopped)
1 leek (finely sliced)
1 tbsp olive oil
3 tbsp butter
30g/¼ cup of plain flour
900g potatoes (thinly sliced)
225g/3 cups of button mushrooms (sliced)
525ml/2 & 1/3 cups of milk
1 tsp Worcestershire sauce
1 tsp wholegrain mustard
Salt & black pepper (to season)

1. Heat the olive oil in a frying pan and add the cubed chicken. Cook until lightly browned. Remove the chicken from the frying pan and leave to one side.

2. Add 2 tbsp butter to the frying pan and melt. Add the chopped leek and fry for about 2-3 minutes. Gradually add the flour over the top of the leeks and remove the heat.

3. Carefully stir in the milk and blend together until smooth. Return to the heat and bring to the boil, stirring continuously.

4. Cook and stir until the mixture is thickened. Remove from the heat.

5. Add in the Worcestershire sauce, mustard, chicken, carrot and mushrooms and mix together well. Season with salt and black pepper, according to taste.

Chicken and Mushroom Bake/Cont.

6. Line the bottom of the slow cooker with a layer of the sliced potatoes, followed by 1/3 of the chicken mixture.

7. Repeat this layering sequence, ending with a layer of potato. Dot the layer of potato with the remaining butter. Cover and cook on a high temperature for 4 hours.

Chicken & Smoked Sausage Casserole (Serves 6)

Ingredients
450g boneless chicken thighs (skinless & diced)
335ml/1½ cups of chicken broth
225g cooked smoked sausage (sliced)
1 green pepper (chopped)
110g cooked ham (diced)
450g/2 cups of canned chopped tomatoes
170g/¾ cups of tomato puree
150g/1 cup of onion (chopped)
60ml/¼ cup of water
1 tsp Creole seasoning (or to taste)
Dash of hot pepper sauce
250g/2 cups of cooked rice

Method

1. Cook at a low temperature. Place the chicken, sausage, ham, onion, chopped tomatoes, tomato puree, broth, seasoning and hot pepper sauce in the slow cooker and gently mix together.

2. Cover and cook for 6 hours. Add the green pepper and rice 10 minutes before the end of cooking.

Spiced Crockpot Chicken (Serves 6)

Ingredients chicken:

Ingredients marinade:

6 chicken breasts (skinless)
60ml/¼ cup of cold water
60ml/¼ cup of semi-skimmed milk
225g/3 cups of mushrooms (sliced)
1 red bell pepper (sliced)
¼ tsp ground ginger
3 tbsp cornstarch
2 tbsp butter
300g/1 & 1/3 cup of canned mandarin oranges (drained)

170g/¾ cup of tomato puree
450ml/2 cups of chicken broth
2 tbsp soy sauce
2 tbsp brown sugar
1/8 tsp ginger
2 cloves of garlic (crushed)
1 tsp salt

Method

1. Place the marinade ingredients in a bowl and mix together well. Add the chicken breasts to the marinade; cover and refrigerate for 8 hours, (or overnight.)

2. Cook at a low temperature. Remove from the refrigerator and place the chicken in the base of the slow cooker; cover with the marinade.

3. Place the butter in non-stick frying pan and sauté the sliced mushrooms for 2-3 minutes. Add to the slow cooker.

4. Place the lid on the slow cooker and place in the oven for 6 hours.

5. An hour before the end of cooking, stir in the red pepper slices, ginger and mandarin orange segments. Continue to cook for the remaining hour.

6. Place the milk, cold water and cornstarch in a mixing jug and mix together well.

7. Gradually stir the mixture into the slow cooker; cover with the lid and return to the oven for 15-20 minutes.

Creamy Chicken and Mushroom Crockpot (Serves 4)

Ingredients
4 chicken breasts (skinless & chopped)
335ml/1½ cup of cream of chicken & mushroom soup
300g/4 cups of mushrooms (sliced)
Salt & black pepper (to season)
Chopped parsley (to garnish)

Method

1. Cook at a low temperature. Spray the inside of the slow cooker with low-fat cooking spray.

2. Place the chicken in the slow cooker and cover with the soup and mushrooms; season with salt and black pepper.

3. Cover with the lid and cook for 6-8 hours, (stirring halfway through cooking).

4. Garnish with the chopped parsley. Serve with potatoes and vegetables, or alternatively hot rice.

Dijon Chicken with Spinach (Serves 8)

Ingredients

8 chicken breasts (skinless)
Salt & black pepper (to season)
1 heaped tbsp Dijon mustard
750g baby spinach
4 tbsp butter (cut into pieces)

Method

1. Cook at a low temperature. Spray the slow cooker with non-stick cooking spray.

2. Rub the chicken breasts with the Dijon mustard and season with salt and pepper.

3. Place the chicken in the slow cooker and top with the baby spinach. Dot the butter equally over the top of the spinach – and season with salt and pepper.

4. Cover and cook for 5 to 6 hours.

Flavour-Rich Slow-Cook Chicken (Serves 6)

Ingredients
6 chicken breasts (skinless)
2 cloves of garlic (crushed)
4 tbsp dry sherry
½ cup of soy sauce
½ cup of honey
1 inch of fresh ginger root (finely chopped)
2 tbsp cornstarch

Method

1. Cook at a low temperature. Place the soy sauce, ginger, honey, sherry and garlic in a bowl and mix together.

2. Place the chicken breasts in the slow cooker and pour the sauce over the top. Cover and cook for 6 to 7 hours.

3. Transfer the chicken only to a warm serving dish. Keep warm. Pour the sauce into a frying pan and blend the cornstarch with a little water in a mixing jug.

4. Stir the cornstarch mixture into the sauce and cook over a medium heat until thickened. Pour a little of the sauce over the chicken. Serve with hot cooked rice.

Herbed Chicken in Cider (Serves 6)

Ingredients
6 chicken breasts (skinless)
450g shallots
4 cloves of garlic (peeled, but not sliced or crushed)
500ml/2¼ cups of dry cider
335g/1½ cups of crème fraiche
2 bay leaves
2 tbsp fresh tarragon (chopped)
1 tbsp fresh parsley (chopped)
2 tbsp vegetable oil
Salt & black pepper (to season)

Method

1. Place the shallots in a large bowl and pour over with boiling water, enough to cover them. Leave to stand for 15 minutes. Drain and peel off the skins. Heat the vegetable oil in the frying pan and add the shallots, (whole). Fry gently for 8-10 minutes, until lightly browned.

2. Cook at a low temperature. Add the garlic and fry for a further 3 minutes. Remove from the heat and transfer the garlic and shallots to the slow cooker, (do not pour in the oil.)

3. Place the frying pan and oil back over the heat and add the chicken. Cook for 3-4 minutes until lightly browned on both sides. Place the chicken over the shallots and garlic in the slow cooker.

4. Add the cider and bay leaves to the frying pan and bring to the boil. Season with salt and black pepper, according to taste. Pour the cider into the slow cooker. Cover and cook for 4½ to 5 hours, until the chicken and shallots are cooked. Remove the chicken breasts from the slow cooker and keep warm.

5. Stir the herbs and crème fraiche into the cider mixture in the slow cooker and mix well. Return the chicken breasts to the slow cooker and cook on a high temperature for a further 30 minutes.

6. Remove the bay leaves and garlic cloves before serving. Serve with a choice of fresh vegetables and potatoes.

Hot 'n' Spicy BBQ Chicken (Serves 4)

Ingredients
4 chicken breasts (skinless)
1 clove of garlic (crushed)
2 tbsp cider vinegar
1½ tsp ground red-hot pepper flakes
1½ tomato ketchup
2 tbsp brown sugar
1 tbsp Worcestershire sauce
1 tbsp soy sauce

Method

1. Cook at a low temperature. Place all the ingredients, (except the chicken), in the slow cooker and mix together well. Add the chicken breasts and coat well with the sauce.

2. Cover and cook for 4 hours, until the chicken is cooked through. Serve with rolls or as part of a BBQ meal.

Lemon Chicken (Serves 8)

Ingredients
6-8 chicken breasts (skinless and chopped)
110ml/½ cup of dry white wine
2 tsp oregano
6 tbsp lemon juice
2 cloves of garlic
2 tbsp butter
Salt & black pepper (to season)

Method

1. Cook at a low temperature. Place the chopped chicken in a bowl and add half of the oregano and garlic; coating all the chicken. Season with salt and pepper.

2. Melt the butter in a non-stick frying pan and add the chicken. Cook until browned. Remove from the heat and place the chicken in the slow cooker.

3. Add the remaining garlic and oregano, followed by the dry white wine. Cover and cook for 6-8 hours; adding the lemon juice for the final hour of cooking.

Prawn Chicken (Serves 4-6)

Ingredients

400g chicken breast (skinless & diced)
450g large prawns (deveined, tailed and peeled)
150g/1 cup of onion (chopped)
40ml/½ cup of white wine
2 cloves of garlic (crushed)
335ml/1½ cups of sieved tomatoes (passata)
2 tsp vegetable oil
15g/¼ cup of fresh parsley (chopped)
1 tsp dried basil

Method

1. Cook at a low temperature. Heat the vegetable oil in a large non-stick frying pan and add the diced chicken. Cook until lightly browned and then transfer to the slow cooker.

2. Add the garlic, onion and parsley to the frying pan and sauté for 1-2 minutes. Remove from the heat and add the sieved tomatoes, white wine and basil; stir well and pour over the chicken in the slow cooker.

3. Cover and cook for 5 hours. Add the prawns, stirring in gently. Cook for a further 1½ hours. Once cooked, serve with hot rice or noodles.

Spiced Cranberries & Chicken (Serves 8)

Ingredients

8-10 chicken breasts (skinless)
200g/2 cups of fresh cranberries
2 onions (chopped)
450ml/2 cups of orange juice
6 tbsp honey
½ tsp ground ginger
½ tsp ground cinnamon
1 tsp salt
3 tbsp flour (mixed with 2 tbsp cold water)

Method

1. Cook at a low temperature. Place all of the ingredients, (except the flour mixture), in the slow cooker and gently mix.

2. Cover and cook for 7 hours, until the chicken is cooked through. Stir in the flour mixture and cook for a further 20 minutes, or until the mixture has thickened. Serve with a choice of vegetables.

Smoked Paprika Chicken & Potatoes (Serves 4)

Ingredients

4 chicken breasts (skinless)
2 tbsp Spanish smoked paprika
1 onion (sliced)
2 carrots (sliced)
375g/5 cups of small white potatoes (peeled & cut into 1 inch pieces)
1 tsp Worcestershire sauce
1 tbsp fresh parsley (chopped)
1 tbsp honey
1 tbsp lemon juice
3 tbsp melted butter
Salt & pepper (to season)
Pinch of cumin

Method

1. Cook at a low temperature. Place the carrots, onion, potatoes and parsley in the slow cooker and season with the salt and pepper.

2. Add 1½ tablespoons of the butter and combine well. Place the remaining butter, lemon juice, Worcestershire sauce, honey, smoked paprika and pinch of cumin.

3. Rub the chicken breasts well with the mixture and place on top of the vegetables in the slow cooker.

4. Cover and cook for 7 to 8 hours, or until the chicken is cooked through.

Chicken

Sweet & Sour Chicken (Serves 6)

Ingredients

6 chicken breasts (skinless)
350g jarred sweet & sour sauce
400g/2 cups of canned pineapple chunks (drained)
5 carrots (chopped)
40g/¼ cup of onion (chopped)
85g/½ cup of green pepper (chopped)
2 tbsp cornstarch
Salt & black pepper (to season)

Method

1. Cook at a low temperature. Place all the ingredients, (except the chicken & cornstarch), in the slow cooker and gently mix together. Place the chicken breasts over the top and cover. Cook for 7 to 8 hours.
Transfer the chicken only to a warm serving dish. Keep warm.

2. Blend the cornstarch with a little cold water and stir into the liquid in the slow cooker. Stir until thickened. Pour the sauce over the chicken and serve over hot cooked rice.

Italian-Style Mozzarella Chicken (Serves 8)

Ingredients

8 chicken breasts (skinless)
280g/1¼ cups of sieved tomatoes (passata)
170g/¾ cup of tomato puree
100g/1 cup of grated mozzarella cheese
2 cloves of garlic (crushed)
2 tsp oregano
Salt & black pepper (to season)
3 tbsp water
Grated Parmesan cheese (to serve)

Method

1. Cook at a low temperature. Season the chicken with salt and pepper and place in the slow cooker.

Italian-Style Mozzarella Chicken/Cont.

2. Place the tomato puree, sieved tomatoes, garlic, oregano and water in a bowl and combine well. Pour over the chicken in the slow cooker, cover and cook for 7 to 8 hours.

3. Transfer the chicken only to a warm serving dish. Keep warm. Increase the slow cooker temperature to a high setting.

4. Stir the mozzarella cheese into the cooked sauce and cook until the cheese is fully melted.

5. Serve the chicken over hot cooked pasta and pour the hot sauce over the top. Sprinkle with Parmesan cheese.

Fish

Hot Prawn Soup Thai-Style (Serves 4)

Ingredients

450g uncooked king prawns (peeled & de-veined)
225g canned sliced mushrooms (drained)
3 red chillies (deseeded & sliced)
900ml/4 cups of hot chicken stock
3 lemon grass stalks
3 tbsp Thai fish sauce
3 tbsp fresh lime juice
1 tbsp fresh coriander leaves
2 tbsp spring onions (chopped)
Salt & black pepper (to season)

Method

1. When peeling the king prawns, reserve the shells. Place the peeled and de-veined king prawns in the refrigerator and rinse the shells under the cold running water.

2. Place the shells in the slow cooker and pour in the chicken stock. Cover and set to a high temperature.

Hot Prawn Soup Thai-Style/Cont.

3. Bruise the end of the lemon grass stalks with a pestle, or another suitable kitchen implement. Add the stalks to the slow cooker, stirring well. Cook for 2 hours.

4. Strain the stock onto a large bowl, discarding the shells and lemon grass stalks. Rinse out the slow cooker.

5. Pour the drained stock back into the slow cooker and add in the mushrooms. Cook for a further 30 minutes.

6. Add the king prawns and cook for 10-15 minutes, until pink and cooked.

7. Stir the lime juice, fish sauce, coriander, chillies and spring onions into the soup. Season with salt and black pepper, according to taste.

Fish Pie (Serves 8)

Ingredients

800g haddock fillet (skinned & cut into pieces)
225g peeled cooked prawns
250g/1 cup of canned sweet corn (drained)
225g/1½ cups of frozen peas
50g/1 cup of fresh wholemeal breadcrumbs
100g/1 cup of Cheddar cheese (grated)
225g/1 cup of cream cheese
300ml/1 & 1/3 cups of milk
4 tbsp cornstarch
Salt & black pepper (to season)

Method

1. Cook at a high temperature. Place the haddock pieces in a large bowl and sprinkle in the cornstarch. Coat all of the pieces evenly. Add in the peas, prawns and sweet corn and combine well.

2. Place the milk and cream cheese in a separate bowl and blend together. Season with salt and black pepper and stir in.

3. Pour over the fish and vegetable mixture. Transfer into the slow cooker. Cover and cook for 2 to 2½ hours.

4. Place the grated cheese and breadcrumbs in a bowl and mix together well.

5. Remove the cooking pot from the slow cooker and spoon the breadcrumb mixture evenly over the fish.

6. Place under a medium heat grill for 5 minutes, until golden brown. Serve immediately.

Fish

Tuna Casserole with Beans (Serves 4)

Ingredients
225g/1 cup of canned tuna in springwater, (drained & flaked)
450g/6 cups of small white beans (soaked overnight & drained)
2 cloves of garlic (crushed)
560g/2½ cups of canned chopped tomatoes
2.5 litres/6 cups of water
4 tbsp olive oil
1 tsp dried basil
Salt & black pepper (to season)

Method

1. Cook at a high temperature. Heat the oil in a frying pan and add the garlic. Sauté for 3-5 minutes, until golden brown. Discard the garlic and transfer the garlic flavoured oil to the slow cooker.

2. Add the white beans and the water to the slow cooker and stir in with the oil. Cover and cook for 2 hours.

3. Reduce the slow cooker to a low temperature and continue to cook for 7 hours. Return the slow cooker heat to a high temperature. Add the tomatoes, tuna, herbs and season with salt and black pepper.

4. Re-cover and cook for a further 30 minutes.

Salmon Risotto (Serves 8)

Ingredients

900g salmon fillet (skinned & diced)
Bunch of spring onions (finely sliced)
450g/2 cups of easy-cook Arborio rice
280ml/1¼ cups of white wine
2.75 litres/6½ cups of vegetable stock
1 small cucumber (peeled & chopped)
1 small radish (finely chopped)
3 tbsp fresh tarragon (chopped)
3 tbsp butter (melted)
Salt & black pepper (to season)

Method

1. Cook at a high temperature. Add the melted butter to the slow cooker, followed by the chopped spring onions, radish and cucumber. Cover and cook for 25-35 minutes.

2. Stir in the rice, followed by the white wine and vegetable stock. Re-cover and cook for 45 minutes, stirring halfway through cooking.

3. Stir in the salmon and season well with salt and black pepper. Re-cover and cook for a further 15 minutes, until the rice and salmon are cooked.

4. Stand for 5-10 minutes, open and gently stir in the tarragon. Serve immediately

Fish

Seafood Jambalaya (Serves 4)

Ingredients
225g haddock (boned, skinned & cubed)
115g cooked prawns
110g cooked chicken (diced)
6 rashers of streaky bacon (chopped)
750ml/3 & 1/3 cups of hot vegetable stock
1 onion (chopped)
2 cloves of garlic (crushed)
4 tomatoes (skinned & chopped)
2 celery sticks (chopped)
1 green pepper (deseeded & chopped)
1 tsp cayenne pepper
300g easy-cook rice
1 tbsp tomato puree
2 bay leaves
1 tsp dried thyme
1 tsp dried oregano
2 tbsp vegetable oil

Method

1. Heat the oil in a frying pan and add the bacon. Cook for 2-3 minutes. Add the onion, pepper and celery and cook for a further 6-8 minutes, until softened. Pour into the slow cooker.

2. Add the tomato puree, hot vegetable stock, thyme, oregano, garlic, cayenne pepper and bay leaves to the slow cooker and stir together well. Cover and cook on a high heat for 1 hour.

3. Add the rice to the slow cooker, followed by the haddock pieces.

4. Season well with salt and black pepper and re-cover; continue to cook for 40-45 minutes.

5. Stir in the prawns and cook for a further 15 to 20 minutes, until the fish and rice are tender, (do not overcook the rice).

Salmon in White Wine (Serves 4)

Ingredients
900g salmon fillets
300ml/1 & 1/3 cups of dry white wine
Juice of 1 lemon
Grated rind of 1 lemon
2 bay leaves
1 tsp fresh parsley (chopped)
1 tbsp olive oil
Salt & black pepper (to season)

Method

1. Grease the slow cooker with the olive oil. Lay the salmon in the base of the slow cooker and add the white wine, parsley, bay leaves, lemon rind and juice and season with salt and black pepper.

2. Cover and cook on a low temperature for 3 to 4 hours. Serve with a green salad.

Fish

Shrimp in Marinara Sauce (Serves 6)

Ingredients

675g cooked shrimp (shelled & de-veined)
620g/2¾ cups of canned chopped tomatoes
225g/1 cup of tomato puree
2 cloves of garlic (crushed)
½ tsp basil
1 tsp oregano
½ tsp black pepper
½ tsp salt
2 bay leaves
1 tsp fresh parsley (chopped)
Grated Parmesan cheese (to serve)

Method

1. Cook at a low temperature. Place the tomato puree, chopped tomatoes, garlic, basil, oregano, salt, black pepper and parsley in the slow cooker. Combine well.

2. Cover and cook for 5 to 6 hours. Increase the slow cooker to a high temperature. Add the cooked shrimp and stir into the sauce. Cook for a further 20 minutes. Remove the bay leaves.

3. Serve with hot cooked spaghetti and sprinkle with Parmesan cheese.

Lamb

Herbed Lamb Shanks (Serves 4)

Ingredients
4 lamb shanks
1 carrot (finely chopped)
200g/1 cup of brown lentils
2 celery sticks (finely chopped)
2 cloves of garlic (crushed)
110ml/½ cup of red wine
400g/1¾ cup of canned chopped tomatoes, with herbs
2 tsp mixed herbs
2 tsp minced chilli
Salt & black pepper (to season)

Method

1. Cook at a low temperature. Place the lamb shanks in the slow cooker.

2. Place the celery, carrot, garlic, lentils, herbs, chopped tomatoes, wine and chilli in a bowl and mix together. Pour over the lamb shanks in the slow cooker.

3. Cover and cook for 9 to 10 hours, stirring halfway through, (preferred, but not essential).

4. Season with salt and black pepper and serve with mashed potato.

Rustic Lamb Stew (Serves 4-6)

Ingredients

1.25kg stewing lamb (cubed)
400g/1¾ cup of canned chopped tomatoes
2 tbsp plain flour
2 cloves of garlic (crushed)
4 tbsp olive oil
170ml/¾ cup of dry white wine
150ml/2/3 cup of lamb stock
1 sprig of fresh rosemary
½ tsp salt
Salt & black pepper (to season)

Method

1. Cook at a high temperature. Place the flour in a bowl and season with some black pepper. Toss the lamb in the flour, coating each piece well.

2. Heat the oil in a pan and add the lamb. Cook for 4-5 minutes, until lightly browned. Transfer to the slow cooker.

3. Add the garlic to the pan and cook for 1 minute, followed by the lamb stock and white wine. Bring to the boil, stirring continuously.

4. Pour over the lamb in the slow cooker. Stir in the tomatoes and season with salt and black pepper. Cover and cook for 1 to 1½ hours.

5. Reduce the heat to low and continue to cook for 6 to 8 hours, until the lamb is tender. Serve with warm crusty bread.

Lamb

Lamb Casserole with Haricot Beans (Serves 6)

Ingredients

500g boned lamb shoulder (trimmed & cubed)
300g piece of boiling bacon (cubed)
6 pork sausages (chopped)
1 onion (chopped)
2 cloves of garlic (crushed)
2 celery sticks (chopped)
200g/3 cups of white haricot beans
400g/cups of canned chopped tomatoes
450ml/2 cups of water
150g/2/3 cup of tomato puree
50g butter
1 beef stock cube (crumbled)
100g/2 cups of soft breadcrumbs
1 tsp dried thyme
1 tsp allspice
1 tbsp vegetable oil
¼ cup of fresh parsley (chopped)

Method

1. Cook at a high temperature. Heat the oil in a frying pan and add the cubed lamb. Cook until lightly browned, remove from the heat and drain. Transfer to the slow cooker.

2. Place the onion, bacon, garlic, celery, haricot beans, sausage, tomato puree, allspice, thyme, stock cube and chopped tomatoes in the slow cooker and gently mix together.

Lamb

3. Cover and cook for 8 to 10 hours, stirring halfway through cooking, (preferred, but not essential). Season the casserole with salt.

4. Heat the butter in a frying pan and add the breadcrumbs. Cook until the breadcrumbs are golden brown.

5. Serve the casserole in serving dishes, sprinkled with the breadcrumbs and garnished with chopped parsley.

Sweet Lamb Curry (Serves 6)

Ingredients
950g lamb (cubed)
3 cloves of garlic (crushed)
1 onion (chopped)
60g/½ cup of desiccated coconut
300ml/1 & 1/3 cup of canned coconut milk
3 tbsp sliced fresh lemongrass
1¼ tbsp minced chilli
2 tbsp minced ginger
1 tsp turmeric
1 tsp cumin
Salt (to season)
Fresh coriander (chopped)

Method

1. Cook at a low temperature. Heat the oil in a frying pan and add the cubed lamb. Cook until lightly browned, remove from the heat and drain. Transfer to the slow cooker.

2. Add the remaining ingredients, (except the coriander), and gently stir together.

3. Cover and cook for 9 to 10 hours. Serve with hot rice, garnished with chopped coriander.

Lancashire Lamb Hot-Pot (Serves 4-6)

Ingredients
8 lamb chops (trimmed)
75g/1 cup of button mushrooms (sliced)
875g/5 cups of potatoes (thinly sliced)
2 carrots (sliced)
2 onions (sliced)
1 leek (sliced)
1 celery stick (sliced)
500ml/2¼ cups of lamb stock
1 tsp mixed herbs
Sprig of fresh rosemary
1 tbsp butter (melted)
Salt & black pepper (to season)

Method

1. Place a layer of potato slices on the base of the slow cooker and top with a mixed layer of the sliced vegetables.

2. Sprinkle over with a little of the mixed herbs and season with salt and black pepper. Place 4 lamb chops over the top.

3. Repeat this potato, vegetable, meat and seasoning layer, then continue to layer with potato and vegetables; finishing with a layer of potato on top.

4. Pour the lamb stock into the slow cooker and cover. Cook on a high temperature for 1 hour. Reduce the temperature to low and continue to cook for 6 to 8 hours.

5. To brown the top, brush the top of the potatoes with melted butter and place under a medium grill for 4-5 minutes.

Lamb

Lamb Shepherd's Pie (Serves 4-6)

Ingredients
500g lamb mince
1 onion (finely chopped)
875g/5 cups of potatoes (diced)
2 carrots (finely chopped)
2 celery sticks (finely chopped)
2 tbsp butter
1 tbsp cornstarch
4 tbsp milk
2 tbsp fresh rosemary (chopped)
1 tbsp Worcestershire sauce
225ml/1 cup of hot lamb stock
Salt & black pepper (to season)

Method

1. Cook at a high temperature. Heat a large non-stick frying pan and add the lamb mince. Cook until lightly browned.

2. Add the carrots, onion and celery and cook for a further 2-3 minutes.

3. Dissolve the cornstarch in a small bowl with a little water and stir into the lamb stock. Pour into the frying pan and bring to the boil.

4. Remove from the heat and stir in the Worcestershire sauce and rosemary. Season with salt and black pepper and transfer the mixture to the slow cooker.

5. Cover and cook for 2½ to 3 hours. 30 minutes before the end of the cooking time, place the potatoes in a pan of boiling water and cook until tender.

6. Drain and mash, stirring in the milk and butter. Spoon the mashed potatoes on top of the lamb and spread evenly, pressing the top down with a fork.

7. Re-cover and cook for a further 45 minutes.

Lamb with Sour Cream Sauce (Serves 6)

Ingredients

1.25kg boneless lamb (cubed)
85g/¾ cup of flour
2 tbsp flour
1 large onion (chopped)
395ml/1¾ cup of beef broth
280g/1¼ cup of sour cream
2 tbsp water
½ tsp caraway seed
¼ tsp rosemary leaves (crushed)
2 tbsp vegetable oil
2 tsp salt
1 tsp tarragon vinegar
½ tsp dill seed

Method

1. Spray the slow cooker with non-stick cooking spray, or lightly grease with butter. Cook at a low temperature.

2. Heat the oil in a frying pan and add the cubed lamb. Cook until lightly browned, remove from the heat and drain.

Lamb with Sour Cream Sauce/Cont.

3. Place the salt, $\frac{3}{4}$ cup of flour, dill seed, rosemary and caraway seed in a bowl and mix together. Toss the lamb in the mixture and coat well. Transfer to the slow cooker and stir in the onion, vinegar and beef broth.

4. Cover and cook for 10 to 12 hours. Place the 2 tbsp flour and the water in a measuring jug and mix together.

5. Stir into the slow cooker, re-cover and cook for 20-30 minutes, until thickened. Stir in the sour cream and cook for a further 5 minutes. Serve with hot cooked rice.

Pork

Apple & Cranberry Pork Chops (Serves 8)

Ingredients

8 pork chops
1 cup of cranberry sauce
1 cup of applesauce
3 sweet potatoes (peeled & thinly sliced)
2 tbsp honey
Salt & black pepper (to season)
2 tbsp vegetable oil

Method

1. Cook at a low temperature. Season the pork chops with salt and black pepper, according to taste.

2. Heat the oil in a frying pan and add the chops, cook for a couple of minutes until the chops are lightly browned each side. Remove from the heat.

3. Pour the applesauce into the base of the slow cooker, followed by the sweet potato slices. Drizzle the honey over the sweet potato and season with salt and black pepper.

4. Lay the pork chops over the potato and cover with cranberry sauce. Cover and cook for 7 to 9 hours.

Barbeque-Style Slow-Cook Sausages (Serves 6)

Ingredients

8-10 sausages
400g/1¾ cups of canned chopped tomatoes, with herbs
110ml/½ cup of beef stock
3 tbsp tomato puree
2 tbsp white wine vinegar
2 tbsp brown sugar
1 tbsp mustard
1½ tbsp Worcestershire sauce

Method

1. Cook at a low temperature. Place the sausages in the slow cooker.

2. Place the rest of the ingredients in a large bowl and mix together well. Pour over the sausages. Cover and cook for 7 to 8 hours.

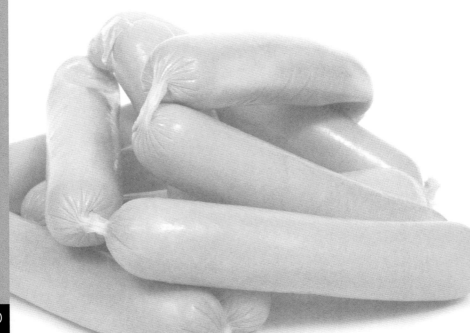

Five-Spice Pork Chinese-Style (Serves 4)

Ingredients

375g pork fillet (trimmed & cubed)
1 tbsp dried Chinese mushrooms
110g baby sweet corn (sliced lengthways in half)
170ml/⅜ cup of hot vegetable stock
200g/1 cup of pineapple chunks (in juice)
1 green pepper (deseeded & sliced)
110g water chestnuts
1 red chilli (deseeded & finely chopped)
1 tsp Chinese five-spice powder
1 inch of fresh root ginger (grated)
1 tbsp dark soy sauce
1 tbsp hoisin sauce
1 tbsp sherry vinegar
4 tsp cornstarch
1 tbsp vegetable oil

Method

1. Cook at a high temperature. Place the dried mushrooms in a bowl and pour in the hot vegetable stock.

2. Leave to soak for 20-25 minutes. Drain, reserving the stock. Slice any large mushrooms in half.

3. Drain the pineapple chunks, reserving the liquid. Place the cornstarch in a bowl and add a little of the reserved pineapple juice, blend together until smooth. Add the remaining juice.

4. Heat the vegetable oil in a frying pan and add the pork. Cook quickly on a high heat, lightly browning both sides

Five-Spice Pork Chinese-Style/Cont.

5. Transfer to the slow cooker, followed by the pineapple chunks, vegetables and water chestnuts.

6. Place the five-spice powder, ginger, chilli powder, soy sauce, hoisin sauce, vinegar and reserved stock in a bowl and mix together well. Add the cornstarch/pineapple juice mixture and combine. Transfer to the frying pan and bring to the boil, stirring continuously.

7. When the mixture in the frying pan thickens, pour into the slow cooker. Cover and cook for 1 hour.

8. Reduce the slow cooker to a low temperature and cook for a further 1½ to 2½ hours, until the pork is tender. Serve with hot rice.

Pork & Black Beans Mexican-Style (Serves 4-6)

Ingredients

450g pork loin (cubed)
870g/14 cups of canned black beans (rinsed & drained)
450g/2 cups of canned chopped tomatoes
1 green pepper (deseeded & chopped)
1 onion (chopped)
1 clove of garlic (crushed)
450ml/2 cups of water
1 tsp chilli powder
1 tsp salt
½ tsp black pepper
1 tsp ground coriander
2 tbsp vegetable oil
Fresh chopped parsley (to serve)

Method

1. Cook at a low temperature.
Place the chilli powder, salt and
coriander in a bowl and add the
pork cubes. Toss the pork,
coating all the pieces well.

2. Heat the oil in a frying pan and
add the onion and garlic. Cook for
3-4 minutes, until lightly browned. Add
to the slow cooker, (without the
heated oil).

3. Add the coated pork to the frying pan and
cook, until lightly browned. Transfer to the slow
cooker, followed by the tomatoes, green pepper, water
and black pepper. Stir together well.

4. Cover and cook for 8 to 9 hours. Serve over hot cooked rice and
garnish with fresh chopped parsley.

Pork Casserole with Fettuccine (Serves 6)

Ingredients

900g pork tenderloin (thinly sliced)
1½ onions (sliced)
225g/1 cup of canned chopped tomatoes (drained)
60g/¼ cup of red wine
170g/¾ cups of sour cream
2 tbsp paprika
1½ tbsp caraway seed
2 tbsp vegetable oil
Salt & black pepper (to season)
¾ lb fettuccine (cooked)

Method

1. Cook at a high temperature. Heat the vegetable oil and add the onions and sliced pork. Cook until the pork is lightly browned.

2. Add the caraway seed, paprika and season with salt and black pepper. Cook for 1 minute. Stir in the red wine and tomatoes and cook for 30-40 seconds.

3. Transfer the mixture to the slow cooker and cook for 3 to 4 hours. Stir in the sour cream, re-cover and cook for 10 minutes. Serve over hot cooked fettuccine.

Pork Chilli (Serves 8)

Ingredients

900g pork loin (cubed)
450g canned chilli beans (undrained)
110g salsa (mild or hot, according to taste)
75g/½ cup of onion (chopped)
1 red pepper (chopped)
845g/3¾ cups of canned chopped tomatoes, in herbs
225g/1 cup of tomato puree
1 jalapeno pepper (minced)
2 cloves of garlic (chopped)
1 tbsp chilli powder
½ tsp cayenne pepper
2 tbsp vegetable oil

Method

1. Cook at a low temperature.Heat the oil in a frying pan and add the onion and garlic. Cook for 3-4 minutes, until lightly browned.

2, Add to the slow cooker, (without the heated oil). Add the cubed pork to the frying pan and cook, until lightly browned.

3. Transfer to the slow cooker, followed by the remaining ingredients. Combine well.

4. Cover and cook for 9 to 10 hours.

Pork in Cranberry Sauce (Serves 4-6)

Ingredients
1.5kg pork loin roast
2 cups of cranberry sauce
1/3 cup of French salad dressing
1 onion (sliced)

Method

1. Cook at a low temperature. Place the cranberry sauce, onion and salad dressing in a bowl and mix together.

2. Place the pork joint in the slow cooker and cover with the cranberry sauce mixture. Cover and cook for 7 to 9 hours.

Spicy Pork Fillets (Serves 6)

Ingredients
3 pork fillets (trimmed & halved)
5 shallots (finely chopped)
60ml/¼ cup of fresh lime juice
1 tsp chilli powder
½ tsp cumin
1 tbsp black or yellow mustard seeds
1 tsp ground turmeric
1 tbsp brown sugar

Method

1. Cook at a low temperature. Place all of the ingredients into the slow cooker, cover and cook for 7 to 8 hours, stirring halfway through cooking.

2. When ready to serve, remove the pork fillets from the slow cooker and slice into 1 inch strips. Serve with hot rice and salad, with the sauce spooned over the top.

Pork and Potato Hot-Pot (Serves 6)

Ingredients
6 boneless pork chops (trimmed)
1.25kg potatoes (thinly sliced)
780ml/3½ cups of vegetable stock
1 onion (finely chopped)
1 clove of garlic (crushed)
100g/1 & 1/3 cup of button mushrooms (sliced)
½ tsp mixed herbs
1½ tbsp vegetable oil
1 tbsp butter
Salt & black pepper (to season)

Method

1. Spray the inside of the slow cooker with non-stick cooking spray, or lightly grease with butter. Preheat to a high temperature.

2. Heat the vegetable oil in a frying pan and add the onion. Cook for 4-5 minutes, until softened. Add the mushrooms and garlic and cook for a further 4-5 minutes. Remove from the heat and stir in the mixed herbs.

3. Transfer half of the mixture to the slow cooker, covered by a layer of the sliced potatoes, making sure that they overlap slightly. Season with salt and black pepper.

4. Lay the chops over the top of the potato, followed by half of the vegetable stock.

5. Repeat the layers of mushroom/garlic mixture, followed by layers of potato until the ingredients are all used; making sure to end with a layer of potato. Dot the potatoes with butter.

6. Cover and cook for 4 to 5 hours, until the meat and potatoes are tender.

7. Place under a medium-heat grill for 6-8 minutes to brown the potatoes at the end of cooking.

Sausage, Bacon and Potato Casserole (Serves 4)

Ingredients

8 large pork sausages
6 slices of bacon (cut into 1 inch pieces)
1 clove of garlic (crushed)
1 onion (chopped)
4 baking potatoes (peeled & thinly sliced)
280ml/1¼ cups of vegetable stock
1 tbsp vegetable oil
¼ tsp fresh sage (chopped)
Salt & black pepper (to season)

Method

1. Cook at a high temperature. Heat the vegetable oil in a frying pan and add the sausages. Gently cook them for 4-5 minutes, until golden brown.

2. Remove the sausages from the frying pan and put to one side. Discard all but approximately 2 teaspoons of fat from the pan.

3. Add the bacon to the frying pan and cook for 2-3 minutes. Add the onion and cook for a further 5-7 minutes, until golden. Add the garlic and cook for 1-2 minutes, then remove the frying pan from the heat.

4. Arrange half of the potato slices in the base of the slow cooker and spoon the bacon/onion mixture over the top. Sprinkle the sage and season with salt and black pepper. Cover with the other half of the potato slices.

5. Pour the vegetable stock over the potato and lay the sausages on top. Cover and cook for 3 to 4 hours, until the sausages are cooked and the potato is tender.

Mushroom, Bacon & Potato Soup (Serves 6-8)

Ingredients

6 rashers of rindless back bacon (cut into 1 inch strips)
12 large, flat brown mushrooms (sliced)
8 medium potatoes (peeled & cut into 2 inch cubes)
2 onions (finely chopped)
2 cloves of garlic (crushed)
1010ml/4½ cups of chicken stock
675ml/3 cups of milk
3 bay leaves
1½ tsp fresh thyme leaves
4½ tbsp flour
2 tbsp fresh parsley (chopped)
Salt & black pepper (to season)
2 tbsp vegetable oil

Method

1. Cook at a high temperature. Heat the oil in a non-stick frying pan and add the garlic, bacon and onion. Sauté for 4-5 minutes and then remove from the heat.

Mushroom, Bacon & Potato Soup/Cont.

2. Place the potatoes, mushrooms, chicken stock, thyme, bay leaves and the onion/garlic/bacon mixture in the slow cooker. Cover and cook for 5-6 hours.

3. Place the flour in a small bowl and mix with a little of the milk to make a smooth paste; add to the slow cooker, followed by the remaining milk. Stir in gently. Cook for a further 2 hours.

4. Season with salt and black pepper, according to taste and garnish with chopped parsley.

Tender Pork Chops in a Creamy Sauce (Serves 6)

Ingredients
6 pork chops
1 onion (sliced)
1 clove of garlic (crushed)
55g/½ cup of plain flour
225g/1 cup of sour cream
450ml/2 cups of boiling chicken stock
2 tbsp plain flour
Salt & black pepper (to season)
2 tbsps vegetable oil

Method

1. Cook at a low temperature. Season the pork chops with salt and black pepper, according to taste.

2. Place ½ cup of flour on a plate, or shallow bowl, and coat each of the pork chops.

3. Heat the oil in a frying pan and add the chops, cook for a couple of minutes until the chops are lightly browned each side.

4. Remove the chops from the frying pan and place in the slow cooker. Add the onions and garlic to the frying pan and cook for 4-5 minutes, until tender. Add to the slow cooker, on top of the pork chops.

5. Pour in the chicken stock, cover and cook for 7 to 8 hours.

6. Transfer the pork chops, (without the liquid), to a warm serving dish and keep warm.

7. Place the sour cream and 2 tablespoons of flour in a bowl and mix together well. Stir into the liquid in the slow cooker. Increase the slow cooker heat to high.

8. Re-cover and cook for 20-30 minutes, until the sauce has thickened. When ready, transfer the pork chops to serving plates and top with the creamy sauce.

Italian Sausage & Pearl Barley Soup (Serves 6)

Ingredients

75g uncooked pearl barley
450g Italian sausage (chopped)
75g/½ cup of onion (finely chopped)
2 cloves of garlic (crushed)
2 tsp Italian seasoning
375g/1 & 2/3 cup of canned chopped tomatoes with herbs
1350ml/6 cups of chicken broth
300g/4 cups of spinach (chopped)
2 large carrots (diced)
1 tbsp vegetable oil

Method

1. Cook at a low temperature. Heat the oil in a frying pan and add the onion and garlic. Sauté for 2-3 minutes and then add the sausage. Cook until the sausage is browned on all sides.

2. Sprinkle over the Italian seasoning and cook for a further 30 seconds. Remove from the heat and drain off any fat.

3. Place the chicken broth, pearl barley, carrot, spinach, chopped tomatoes and sausage mixture in the slow cooker. Cover and cook for 7 to 8 hours.

Vegetables

Lentil & Vegetable Soup (Serves 4)

Ingredients
250g red lentils
1 onion (chopped)
2 celery sticks (chopped)
2 cloves of garlic (crushed)
750ml/3 & 1/3 hot vegetable stock
3 tbsp olive oil
1 carrot (peeled & diced)
1 potato (peeled & diced)
½ tsp cumin
2 bay leaves
½ tsp cayenne pepper
Salt & black pepper (to season)
2 tbsp fresh parsley (chopped)

Method

1. Heat the oil in a frying pan and add the onion. Sauté for 4-5 minutes, until soft.

2. Add the garlic, potato, celery and carrot and cook for a further 5 minutes. Transfer the ingredients to the slow cooker.

3. Add the vegetable stock, lentils and bay leaves and stir in well. Cover and cook for 1 hour at a high temperature.

4. Reduce the slow cooker heat to a low temperature and cook for a further 2-3 hours, until the vegetables and lentils are tender.

5. Remove the bay leaves and discard. Spoon the soup into a food processor and blend until smooth.

6. Pour the soup back into the slow cooker and add the cayenne pepper and cumin. Season with salt and pepper, according to taste.

7. Cover and cook for a further 45 minutes. To serve, garnish with fresh parsley.

Moroccan-Style Spiced Soup (Serves 4-6)

Ingredients

400g canned chickpeas (drained)
1 onion (finely chopped)
2 carrots (finely diced)
1 celery stick (finely diced)
400g/1¾ cups of canned chopped tomatoes
350g/2 cups of new potatoes (finely diced)
1010ml/4½ cups of hot vegetable stock
1 tbsp lemon juice
1 tsp cinnamon
1 tbsp fresh root ginger (grated)
1 tsp turmeric
2 tbsp fresh coriander (chopped)
Salt & black pepper (to season)

Method

1. Place the chopped onion and pour 600ml of the vegetable stock into the slow cooker. Cover and cook for 1 hour at a high temperature.

2. Place the spices and 2 tablespoons of the stock in a bowl and mix together to make a paste. Add to the slow cooker, followed by the remaining stock, celery and carrots.

3. Stir in well and season with salt and black pepper. Cover and cook for 1 hour.

4. Add the potatoes, chopped tomatoes and chickpeas and cook for 4-5 hours.

5. Once cooked, stir in the lemon juice and coriander and serve immediately.

Aubergine Parmigiana (Serves 4-6)

Ingredients

4 aubergines (medium size – cut into ½ inch slices)
800g marinara sauce
400g/4 cups of Mozzarella cheese (sliced)
50g/½ cup of Parmesan cheese
2 eggs
30g/1/3 cup of dry breadcrumbs
3 tbsp flour
75ml/1/3 cup of water
2 tbsp virgin olive oil
2 tbsp vegetable oil

Method

1. Place the sliced aubergines in a bowl in layers – sprinkling salt over each layer. Leave for 30 minutes and then dry the slices on paper kitchen towel.

2. Cook at a low temperature. Place the water, flour and egg in a bowl and whisk together. Dip in the aubergine slices, allowing the excess batter to drip off.

3. Heat the vegetable oil in a frying pan and sauté the aubergine slices, a few at a time, for 30 to 60 seconds.

4. Place the breadcrumbs and Parmesan cheese in a bowl and mix together.

5. Place a layer of ¼ of the aubergine slices, followed by ¼ of the breadcrumb mixture, ¼ of the marinara sauce and ¼ of the Mozzarella cheese.

6. Repeat this layering sequence to make 4 layers, finishing with a layer of Mozzarella.

7. Cover and cook for 4 to 5 hours.

Broccoli & Cheese Casserole (Serves 8)

Ingredients
620g/2¾ cups of broccoli florets
200g/2 cups of grated Cheddar cheese
110ml/½ cup of cream of broccoli soup
35-40g/¼ cup of onion (finely chopped)
½ tsp Worcestershire sauce
¼ tsp black pepper

Method

1. Spray the slow cooker with non-stick cooking spray, or lightly grease with butter.

2. Place one cup of the grated cheese, the chopped onion, soup, broccoli, Worcestershire sauce and pepper and mix together well. Transfer to the slow cooker.

3. Cover and cook for 2 to 3 hours on a high temperature, until the broccoli is just tender. Sprinkle over the remaining cheese and cook for a further 10-15 minutes, until the cheese has melted.

Glazed Carrots (6-8 Servings)

Ingredients
600g/4 cups of carrots (sliced)
4 tbsp orange marmalade
560ml/2½ cups of water
2 tbsp pecan nuts (chopped)
3 tbsp butter
¼ tsp salt

1. Cook at a high temperature. Place the water, salt and sliced carrots in the slow cooker. Cover and cook for 2 to 3 hours, until the carrots are done.

2. Drain the carrots and add the butter, marmalade and pecan nuts. Re-cover and cook for a further 25 to 30 minutes.

Courgette Casserole (Serves 4-6)

Ingredients
4 courgettes (sliced)
1 red onion (chopped)
1 green pepper (sliced into strips)
450g/2 cups of canned chopped tomatoes
50g/½ cup of Parmesan cheese
½ tsp dried basil
1 tbsp vegetable oil
1 tbsp butter
Salt & black pepper (to season)

Method

1. Cook at a low temperature. Heat the oil in a frying pan and add the onion. Cook for 4-5 minutes, until tender. Add to the slow cooker.

2. Place the courgettes, green pepper, chopped tomatoes, (with juices) and basil in the slow cooker. Season with salt and black pepper and stir well.

3. Cover and cook for 2½ to 3 hours. Dot the top of the casserole with the butter and sprinkle over the Parmesan cheese. Re-cover and cook for a further 30-45 minutes.

Broccoli & Cheese Soup (Serves 8)

Ingredients
300g/1 & 1/3 cup of broccoli florets (chopped)
200g/2 cups of grated cheddar cheese
35-40g/¼ cup of chopped onion
150g/2 cups of cooked Chinese noodles
1 tbsp flour
2 tbsp butter
1125ml/5 cups of milk
Salt & black pepper (to season)

Broccoli & Cheese Soup/Cont.

Method

1. Cook at a low heat. Place all of the ingredients in a slow cooker and mix together well.

2. Cover and cook for 3-4 hours, until the broccoli is tender.

Potato & Celery Salad (Serves 6)

Ingredients

1.25kg/7 cups of potatoes (uncooked & cubed)
150g/1½ cups of celery (chopped)
150g/1 cup of onion (chopped)
55ml/¼ cup of cider vinegar
280ml/1¼ cup of water
55g/¼ cup of sugar (granulated)
2 tbsp quick-cook tapioca
2 tsp dried parsley
½ tsp black pepper
1 tbsp vegetable oil

Method

1. Cook at a low temperature. Heat the oil in a frying pan and add the onion. Cook for 3-4 minutes, then add the celery; cook for a further 2-3 minutes.

2. Add to the slow cooker, followed by the potatoes. Gently mix together.

3. Place the vinegar, sugar, water, black pepper, tapioca and parsley in a bowl and combine. Pour over the potato mixture in the slow cooker and mix in well.

4. Cover and cook for 7 to 8 hours, until the vegetables are tender.

Carrot and Coriander Soup (Serves 8)

Ingredients

600g/4 cups of carrots (peeled & chopped)
1½ sticks of celery (chopped)
1½ onions (chopped)
2 tbsp vegetable oil
4 small potatoes (peeled & chopped)
1800ml/8 cups of vegetable stock
300ml/1 & 1/3 cup of milk
3 tsp ground coriander
3 tbsp butter
1 tbsp fresh coriander (chopped)
Salt & black pepper (to season)

Method

1. Cook at a low temperature. Heat the vegetable oil and 2 tbsp of the butter in a pan. Add the onion and sauté for 4 minutes, until softened.

Carrot and Coriander Soup/Cont.

2. Add the chopped celery and potatoes to the frying pan and cook for 2 minutes. Add the chopped carrots and cook for a further 1 minute. Remove from the heat and transfer the contents to a slow cooker.

3. Heat the vegetable stock to boiling point; remove from the heat and pour over the vegetables in the slow cooker. Season with salt and black pepper, according to taste.

4. Cover and place in the oven for 5 hours, until the vegetables are tender. At the end of the cooking time, heat the remaining butter in a frying pan and add the ground coriander; fry for 1 minute, stirring continuously.

5. Reduce the heat slightly and add the fresh coriander, fry for 30-40 seconds and then remove from the heat.

6. Spoon the contents into a food processor, (this will have to be done in more than one batch). Blend until the soup is smooth. Pour into a large saucepan and heat over a medium temperature. Stir in the milk and heat until piping hot. Add more seasoning, if desired. Once heated, serve immediately.

Roasted Red Pepper & Aubergine Pasta-Bake (Serves 4)

Ingredients
6 roasted red peppers (cut into strips)
3 courgettes (cut in half, lengthways)
1 aubergine (cut into 1 inch slices)
400g/1¾ cups of canned chopped tomatoes, with herbs
400g fresh lasagne sheets
250g/2½ cups of ricotta cheese
100g/1 cup of mozzarella cheese (grated)
50g/¼ cup of Parmesan cheese

Method

1. Spray the slow cooker with non-stick cooking spray. Preheat to a low temperature.

2. Place a mixed layer of vegetables on the base of the slow cooker. Pour a layer of tomatoes over the top, topped with a layer of lasagne sheets.

3. Repeat this layer sequence, ending with a layer of tomatoes.

4. Place the Parmesan, mozzarella and ricotta cheese in a bowl and mix together. Sprinkle over the top layer of tomatoes. Cover and cook for 5 to 6 hours.

Onion Soup (Serves 6)

Ingredients
2 large onions (sliced)
1350ml/6 cups of hot beef stock
1 tbsp vegetable oil
½ tsp black pepper
2 bay leaves
¼ tsp thyme
100g/1 cup of Parmesan cheese (grated)
Salt (to season, if desired)

Method

1. Cook at a low temperature. Heat the oil in a frying pan and add the sliced onions. Cook for 4-5 minutes, until browned and tender. Add to the slow cooker.

2. Pour the stock into the slow cooker and add the black pepper, bay leaves and thyme; season with salt, if desired.

3. Cover and cook for 3-4 hours. Remove the bay leaves before serving. Serve with a sprinkling of Parmesan cheese on top.

Spiced Rice with Cashews & Spinach (Serves 4)

Ingredients

280g/1¼ cups of easy-cook brown rice
750ml/3 & 1/3 cups of boiling vegetable stock
150g/2 cups of spinach leaves
75g/½ cup of unsalted cashew nuts (toasted)
1 onion (finely chopped)
2 tbsp vegetable oil
1 tbsp unsalted butter
2 carrots (grated)
1 tsp cumin
2 tomatoes (peeled & chopped)
1 clove of garlic (crushed)
1 onion (finely chopped)
2 tbsp vegetable oil

Method

1. Cook at a high temperature. Heat the butter and vegetable oil in a frying pan and add the onion. Fry for 5-6 minutes, until tender. Add the tomatoes and garlic, cook for a further 2-3 minutes.

2. Add the easy-cook rice and cumin and stir in well. Cook for 10-15 seconds then remove from the heat. Transfer to the slow cooker.

3. Add the carrots and vegetable stock and stir. Season with salt and pepper and stir again. Cover and cook for 1 to 1½ hours.

4. Place the spinach over the rice in the slow cooker, re-cover and cook for a further 30-35 minutes.

5. Stir the spinach into the rice and season again, if desired. Sprinkle the cashew nuts over the rice and serve in individual serving bowls.

Vegetables

Sugar 'n' Spiced Butternut Squash (Serves 4)

Ingredients
1 large butternut squash (quartered & deseeded)
50g/¼ cup of brown sugar
½ tsp ground cinnamon
225ml/1 cup of apple juice
3 tbsp butter (melted)

Method

1. Cook at a low temperature. Place the brown sugar, butter and cinnamon in a small bowl and mix together.

2. Place two of the butternut squash quarters in the slow cooker, (cut-side-upwards.). Drizzle over half of the sugar/butter mix.

3. Place the other two quarters on top of the first two quarters; cut-side-upwards again and drizzle over the remaining sugar/butter mix.

4. Cover and cook for 6 to 8 hours, until the squash is tender.

Vegetables

Chilled Sweet Pepper Soup (Serves 8)

Ingredients Soup:
900ml/ cups of vegetable stock
225ml/1 cup of red wine
1½ onion (finely chopped)
2 cloves of garlic (crushed)
4 red peppers (deseeded & quartered)
1.2kg/6 cups of ripe tomatoes (cut into chunks)
3 tbsp olive oil
¾ tsp caster sugar
Fresh chives (chopped – to garnish)
6-8 tbsp crème fraiche (optional)
Salt & black pepper (to season)

Ingredients Croutons:
4 slices of white bread, a couple of
days old (crusts removed & cubed)
3 tbsp olive oil

Soup:

1. Place each of the red pepper quarters under a medium grill, skin-side-up. Grill until the skins begin to blister. Transfer to a bowl to cool down and cover.

2. Heat the oil in a frying pan and add the garlic and onion. Cook for about 8 minutes, until softened. Transfer to the slow cooker.

3. Remove the skin from the peppers and chop the flesh. Add to the slow cooker, followed by the chopped tomatoes, vegetable stock, red wine and sugar.

4. Cover and cook for 3 to 4 hours, until the vegetables are tender. Once cooked, leave to cool slightly for 10-15 minutes.

5. Ladle the soup into a food processor, (this will need to be done in batches), and blend until smooth. Press through a fine sieve into a large bowl.

6. Leave to cool completely and then refrigerate for 3-5 hours. Season with salt and black pepper, as desired.

Croutons:

7. Heat the olive oil in a frying pan and add the bread cubes. Fry until golden brown. Drain on kitchen paper.

8. Serve on top of the chilled soup with a sprinkling of chopped chives. Add a dollop of crème fraiche, if desired.

Sweet Potato & Garlic Soup (Serves 8)

Ingredients
5 sweet potatoes (peeled & cut into 2cm cubes)
10 cloves of garlic (crushed)
2 onions (chopped)
½ tsp salt
8 cups of vegetable soup
3 tbsp olive oil
Salt & black pepper (to season)

Method

1. Preheat the oven to 200C/400F/Gas mark 6. Place the onions, garlic, oil and salt in a roasting dish and mix together well, making sure that the ingredients are all coated in oil. Place in the oven and bake for 15 minutes.

2. Cook at a high temperature. Remove from the oven and place in the slow cooker; adding the sweet potatoes and vegetable stock. Cover and cook for 7-8 hours.

3. Spoon into a food processor and blend until smooth. Pour into a saucepan and reheat, season with salt and pepper, according to taste.

Vegetables

Stuffed Sweet Peppers (Serves 8)

Ingredients

4 red peppers (halved lengthways & deseeded)
4 yellow peppers (halved lengthways & deseeded)
150g/1 cup of instant couscous
150g/1½ cups of feta cheese (cubed)
100g/2/3 cup of dried apricots (finely chopped)
2/3 cup of hot vegetable stock
4 tsp white wine vinegar
2 tbsp olive oil
6 tomatoes (skinned, deseeded & chopped)
6 tbsp toasted pine nuts
4 tbsp fresh parsley (chopped)
Salt & black pepper (to season)

Method

1. Place the halved peppers in a large bowl and cover with boiling water. Leave to stand for 3-4 minutes, then drain. Keep to one side.

2. Place the couscous in a bowl pour in the hot stock. Leave to stand for 5 minutes. Fluff up the couscous with a fork and stir in the vinegar, pine nuts, apricots, feta cheese, tomatoes and parsley. Season with salt and black pepper, according to taste. Fill the peppers with the couscous mixture, pressing it down gently to really fill the peppers.

4. Place the peppers, (filling-side-up), in the slow cooker. Pour 250ml almost boiling water around them, (don't cover the tops).

5. Cover and cook for 2 to 3 hours, until the peppers are tender. Once cooked, brown a little under a medium grill and serve immediately.

Vegetables

Desserts

Apple & Blackberry Fruit Dessert (Serves 8)

Ingredients

500g/5 cups of blackberries (frozen)
4 apples (peeled & thinly sliced)
30g butter
100g/½ cup of dark brown sugar
2 tsp lemon rind (grated)
125g/2½ cups of soft breadcrumbs
40g/½ cup of toasted slivered almonds
8 tbsp whipped cream

Method

1. Spray the slow cooker with non-stick cooking spray, or grease lightly with butter.

2. Thaw the blackberries and drain; reserving the juice. Place the blackberries and apple slices in a bowl and mix together.

3. Place the brown sugar, breadcrumbs and lemon rind in a bowl and mix together. Melt the butter in a pan and add to the breadcrumb mixture, combine well.

4. Place ¼ of the breadcrumb mixture in the base of the slow cooker and top with 1/3 of the fruit mixture. Continue this layering sequence, finishing with a layer of breadcrumbs.

5. Cover and cook on a low temperature for 5 to 6 hours. Serve in individual bowls, with whipped cream and a sprinkling of almonds.

Baked Apples (Serves 6-8)

Ingredients

6-8 medium to large apples (cored)
3 Clementine oranges (peeled, sectioned & chopped)
75g/½ cup of golden raisins
2-3 tsp cinnamon
¼ cup of cold water
75g/1 cup of Peacan Nuts (optional)

Method

1. Place the chopped orange sections, raisins and cinnamon in a bowl and mix together. Stuff the cored apples with fruit and place in the slow cooker.

2. Add the cold water, (to surround the apples), cover and cook on a low temperature for 7 to 8 hours.

3. Remove from cooker and add peacans for decoration,

Chocolate-Dream Dessert (Serves 6)

Ingredients
350g cooking chocolate (broken into pieces)
170ml/¾ cup of double cream
4 eggs
115g/¾ cup of toasted ground almonds
Icing sugar (to dust)

Method

1. Line the base of the slow cooker with a piece of baking paper. Place the broken chocolate into a bowl and place over a saucepan of hot water. Heat until the chocolate is melted.

2. Place the eggs into a bowl and place over a saucepan of hot water for 4-5 minutes, then beat the eggs until thick.

3. Whip the cream in a separate bowl until it thickens and soft peaks form. Fold the chocolate into the eggs, followed by the cream and almonds.

4. Pour the chocolate mixture into the slow cooker, cover and cook on a low temperature for 3½ to 4 hours, until the cake is set.

5. Allow to cool for 30 minutes. Dust with icing sugar and serve with cream or a scoop of ice-cream.

Coconut & Raspberry Dessert Pie (Serves 4-6)

Ingredients
75g/1 cup of coconut
125g/1 cup of raspberries
4 eggs (medium)
225g/1 cup of sugar
60g/½ cup of flour
170g/1½ cups of flour
2 tsp vanilla extract

Method

1. Line the base of the slow cooker with a piece of baking paper. Place the flour, milk, eggs, sugar, vanilla and coconut in a bowl and mix together well with an electric blender.

2. Stir in the raspberries and pour into the slow cooker. Cover and cook on a low temperature for 2½ to 3½ hours, until the pie has set. Serve warm or cold, with ice-cream or frozen yoghurt.

Rum & Caramel Fondue

Ingredients
400g caramels (bagged)
110g small marshmallows
3 tsp rum
2/3 cup of double cream

Method

1. Place the double cream and caramels in the slow cooker. Cover and cook on a high temperature for 45-55 minutes; until the caramels are melted.

2. Add in the rum and marshmallows and stir well. Re-cover and cook for a further 30 minutes.

3. Serve with wedges of apple, or use as a sauce for ice-cream or other desserts.

Chocolate & Coffee Dessert Pots (Serves 4)

Ingredients
300ml/1 & 1/3 cups of milk
150ml/2/3 cup of double cream
4 egg yolks
120g plain chocolate (broken into pieces)
1 tbsp light brown sugar
1 tsp instant coffee powder
1 tbsp coffee liqueur
Whipped cream (to serve)

Method

1. Place the sugar and instant coffee in a pan and mix together. Stir in the milk and cream and place over a medium heat to dissolve the sugar and coffee. Bring to the boil, stirring continuously.

2. Remove from the heat and stir in the chocolate and coffee liqueur.

3. Place the egg yolks in a bowl and whisk. Gradually whisk in the chocolate/cream mixture, mixing together well.

4. Strain the mixture through a sieve into a large mixing jug and then pour into 4 individual serving pots, or ramekins. Cover each with foil.

5. Place in the slow cooker and pour in enough water to come halfway up the sides of the pots/ramekins. Cover and cook on a high temperature for 2¾ to 3 hours, until the dessert is set.

Desserts

Chocolate & Coffee Dessert Pots/Cont.

6. Remove from the slow cooker and remove the foil, leave to cool. Once cooled, cover and place in the refrigerator for at least 1 hour. Serve with whipped cream, if desired.

Cranberry & Chocolate Pudding (Serves 2)

Ingredients
15g/1/8 cup of cranberries
½ apple (peeled & diced)
150g/¾ cup of dark brown sugar
1 egg (lightly beaten)
¼ cup of butter (softened)
30g/¼ cup of self-raising flour
1½ tbsp cocoa powder (unsweetened)
½ tbsp vegetable oil

Method

1. Grease 2 pudding bowls, (heat resistant), with the vegetable oil and line with baking paper. Pour an inch of hot water into the slow cook and preheat to a high temperature.

2. Place the cranberries and diced apple in a bowl and mix together. Add ½ tablespoon of sugar and stir in. Spoon the mixture equally into the pudding bowls and gently press down a little.

3. Place the eggs, cocoa powder, butter and remaining sugar in a bowl and beat together until smooth. Spoon the mixture over the fruit in the pudding bowls and cover over with foil.

4. Place the bowls in the slow cooker and pour in enough water to cover the sides of the bowls about 2/3 up. Cover and cook for 1¾ to 2 hours, until risen and firm.

5. Remove from the slow cooker and leave to cool for 20 minutes.

6. Turn out onto a serving plate and serve with cream or hot chocolate sauce.

Traditional Bread Pudding (Serves 4-6)

Ingredients

100g/2 cups of bread (cut into triangular quarters)

100g/½ cup of brown sugar

75g/½ cup of raisins

2 eggs (lightly beaten)

500g/2¼ cups of milk

1 tsp cinnamon

1 tsp vanilla

¼ tsp salt

110ml/½ cup of water

Method

1. Place the eggs and milk in a large mixing bowl and whisk together. Add the bread, vanilla, sugar, raisins, cinnamon and salt and combine well.

2. Pour the mixture into a baking, or soufflé dish, (one which will fit into your slow cooker). To keep the dish off the bottom of the slow cooker, use either a metal rack, or make a padded ring out of foil.

3. Add ½ cup of water to the slow cooker and place the baking/soufflé dish on top of the rack, or foil ring. Cover and cook on a high temperature for 1½ to 2½ hours, until the pudding is set.

Peanut Butter & Chocolate Chip Cake (Serves 6-8)

Ingredients

110g smooth peanut butter

115g/1 cup of plain flour

280g/1¼ cup of sugar

110ml/½ cup of milk

¾ cup of chocolate chips

2 tbsp unsweetened cocoa

30g/¼ cup of unsweetened cocoa

450ml/2 cups of boiling water

1 tsp vanilla

2 tbsp vegetable oil

1½ tsp baking powder

Peanut Butter & Chocolate Chip Cake/Cont.

Method

1. Spray the inside of the slow cooker with non-stick cooking spray, or lightly grease with butter.

2. Place ½ a cup of the sugar, baking powder and 2 tablespoons of cocoa powder in a bowl and mix together. Gradually add the milk, vanilla and vegetable oil and stir in well, until smooth. Stir in the chocolate chips.

3. Spoon the batter into the slow cooker. Place the remaining ¾ cup of sugar and ¼ cup of cocoa powder in a bowl and mix together.

4. Place the peanut butter in a mixing jug and stir well. Gradually stir into the cocoa/sugar mixture and mix until smooth.

5. Pour over the top of the cake mix in the slow cooker. Cover and cook on a high temperature for 2 to 2½ hours. Once cooked, uncover and allow to cool for 15-20 minutes before serving.

A

Apple & Blackberry Fruit Dessert, pp 87
Apple & Cranberry Pork Chops, pp 59
Artichoke Hearts & Chicken, pp 23
Aubergine Parmigiana, pp 75

B

Baked Apples, pp 88
Barbeque-Style Slow Cook Sausages, pp 60
Beef & 4-Bean Chilli, pp 7
Beef & Autumn Vegetable Stew, pp 8
Beef & Beer Stew, pp 9
Beef Curry, pp 11
Beef in Red Wine with Dumplings, pp 18
Beef Stir-Fry, pp 10
Beef Stroganoff, pp 15
Broccoli & Cheese Casserole, pp 76
Broccoli & Cheese Soup, pp 77

C

Carrot & Coriander Soup, pp 79
Chicken a la King, pp 24
Chicken and Mushroom Bake, pp 29
Chicken & Smoked Sausage Casserole, pp 30
Chicken Cacciatore, pp 24
Chicken Casserole & Wild Rice, pp 25
Chicken Curry, pp 26
Chicken Enchilada Crockpot, pp 27
Chicken Crockpot with Butter Beans, pp 28
Chilli Beef, pp 14
Chilled Sweet Pepper Soup, pp 84
Chocolate Coffee Dessert Pots, pp 91
Chocolate Dream Dessert, pp 89
Coconut & Raspberry Dessert Pie, pp 90
Corned Beef Hash & Cheese Casserole, pp 12
Courgette Casserole, pp 77
Creamy Chicken & Mushroom Crockpot, pp 32

F

Fish Pie, pp 45
Five-Spice Pork Chinese Style, pp 61
Flavour-Rich Slow-Cook Chicken, pp 34

G

Glazed Carrots, pp 76

H

Herbed Chicken in Cider, pp 34
Herbed Lamb Shanks, pp 51
Hot and Spicy BBQ Chicken, pp 36
Hot Beef & Vegetables with Horseradish, pp 16
Hot Prawn Soup, Thai-Style, pp 43

I

Italian-Style Mozzarella Chicken, pp 41
Italian Sausage & Pearl Barley Soup, pp 72

L

Lamb & Sour Cream Sauce, pp 57
Lamb Casserole with Haricot Beans, pp 53
Lamb Shepherd's Pie, pp 56
Lancashire Lamb Hot-Pot, pp 55
Lemon Chicken, pp 36
Lentil & Vegetable Soup, pp 73

M

Mexican Style Meatloaf, pp 13
Moroccan Style Spiced Soup, pp 74
Mushroom, Bacon & Potato Soup, pp 69

O

Onion Soup, pp 81

P

Peanut Butter & Choc-Chip Cake, pp 93
Pork & Black Beans Mexican-Style, pp 63
Pork & Potato Hot-Pot, pp 67
Pork Casserole with Fettuccine, pp 64
Pork Chilli, pp 65
Pork in Cranberry Sauce, pp 66
Potato & Celery Salad, pp 78
Prawn Chicken, pp 37

R

Roasted Red Pepper Pasta Bake, pp 80
Rum & Caramel Fondue, pp 90
Rustic Lamb Stew, pp 52

S

Salmon Risotto, pp 47
Salmon in White Wine, pp 49
Sausage, Bacon & Potato Casserole, pp 68
Seafood Jambalaya, pp 48
Shrimp in Marinara Sauce, pp 50
Smoked Paprika Chicken & Potatoes, pp 39
Spiced Beef in Guinness, pp 20
Spiced Cranberries & Chicken, pp 38
Spiced Crockpot Chicken, pp 31
Spiced Rice with Cashews & Spinach, pp 82
Spicy Pork Fillets, pp 66
Steak & Kidney Pie, pp 19
Stuffed Sweet Peppers, pp 86
Sugar 'n' Spice Butternut Squash, pp 83
Sweet & Sour Chicken, pp 41
Sweet Lamb Curry, pp 54
Sweet Potato & Garlic Soup, pp 85

T

Tender Pork Chops in a Creamy Sauce, pp 70
Three Spice Brisket, pp 21
Traditional Bread Pudding, pp 93
Tuna Casserole with Beans, pp 46